5 TWISTED YEARS

BRITISH COLUMBIA: WHAT REALLY HAPPENED

Editorial Cartoons by **ADRIAN RAESIDE**

Sono Nis Press • Victoria • British Columbia • 1991

Canadian Cataloguing in Publication Data

Raeside, Adrian, 1957-
  Five twisted years

  ISBN 1-55039-003-1

  1. Canada—Politics and government—1984-   —
Caricatures and cartoons.*   2. British Columbia—
Politics and government—1975-   —Caricatures
and cartoons.*   3. World politics—1985-1991—
Caricatures and cartoons.   4. Canadian wit
and humor, Pictorial.   I. Title.

NC1449.R33A4 1991   741.5'971   C90-091676-1

Cover by Adrian Raeside

Most of the cartoons in this book previously
appeared in the Victoria *Times Colonist*.

Published by
SONO NIS PRESS
1745 Blanshard Street
Victoria, British Columbia
Canada   V8W 2J8

Printed in Canada by
MORRISS PRINTING COMPANY LTD.
Victoria, British Columbia

Preface

This book is a record of the last five years. Five rather bizarre years in BC politics. Similar to the five years before that and the five before that, etc. . . . Our unusual political climate and the fact that most BC politicians look like extras from the movie "Deliverance" means that for a political cartoonist, this province is as close as I am probably going to get to heaven.

It's been a long time since I ripped off the book-buying public with a Raeside collection. Not long enough, you say. But hey, this is an unusual historical record. Unusual in that it is drawn rather than written, and unusual because any written words are probably spelled wrong. This book is the product of many 5 o'clock mornings, shackled to a booger-encrusted, ink-stained drawing board, grinding out the only protection we have from the elected hordes . . . an editorial cartoon. The only defence against these bastards is to deflate their enormous egos. No politician will ever admit that a cartoon bothers them. But, as we all know, politicians lie.

A good editorial cartoon should be able to simplify even the most complicated issue and get a laugh at the same time. We live in depressing times. Assassinations, floods, wars, food banks,

Rita Johnston. I try not to stand on a soap box and flog my own political views. I try not to change someone's mind on an issue. All I do is bring the issue to the fore, stripped of all the tawdry trappings, in the most humorous way I can. I try to bring a little levity to an otherwise grim situation. Sometimes that isn't always possible. If all else fails, page four makes a fabulous fire starter.

I have been accused of being cruel and unfair to politicians. Kicking them when they're down. Sure. How many cartoonists close down hospital beds? How many cartoonists reduce welfare payments? How many cartoonists invade other countries? Cartoonists react to the chaos created by elected officials, who slobber all over you until they get your vote. Once they are elected and get caught with their snouts jammed in the trough, turn around and complain about unfair media attention.

Looking back on the last five years of my work, it would be easy to assume that British Columbia, along with the rest of the world, is going to hell in a handcart. You're right, we are. We've been doing that for the last three million years. But we're still around. Putting it into perspective, I am sure the North American Indians were just as horrified to see the first Europeans wade ashore as some Canadians were when the Tamil refugees hit the beach. Our latest crisis is just one of a billion previous crises. This is compounded by the fact that politicians are an unoriginal lot and have a habit of repeating their screw-ups roughly every five years. Makes my job more difficult, as I have to rummage through my old cartoons to make sure I am not plagiarizing myself.

Hopefully, at this point, the store clerk has embarrassed you into buying this book, so I don't have to bother anymore pretending that I can write.

Cheers!

Adrian Raeside

*To my mother, from whom I got my
sense of humour.*

Introduction by a friend

I only know one cartoonist—Adrian Raeside—at all well but somehow I think that's enough. He has been my friend over twelve years now and I believe he is a national treasure, an artful historian who is recording us as we really are, in contrast to who we claim to be. But still, one like him bowling briefly through your work-day life is plenty.

It has to do with sanity and honesty. I am a born conservative, which means I can only handle honesty in manageable portions. Adrian, on the other hand, has contempt for the traditional view of sanity and apparently an unbounding appetite for something closer to the bedrock truths of this world.

He phones almost every weekday. Listening to Raeside ponder aloud and staccato on the outrages and absurdities of each new day, in Victoria and around the world, a process wherein those images begin to coalesce in his fevered mind, is probably like watching brain surgery from the visitors' gallery: mysterious, quite terrifying, but fascinating, infinitely fascinating.

About sanity and honesty: I badly want this world to make sense, don't you? I eagerly look for signs, tracks in the sands of time, which confirm our

world society is marching, slowly perhaps but steadily, towards something immeasurably better. When the signs disappear, I'm not above making them up. Do you ever do that?

Adrian erases them. With his daily quick sketches, he says to me: dream your dreams but this is how it still is. We are often cruel, we are regular liars, we are greedy, stupid and we are frequently absurd. We may be on the road to the New Jerusalem but check the map, we're still in Victoria.

Such integrity, presented as cartoon, is manageable. Most of the time. Thank you, Adrian.

Don Vipond,
Editorial Page Editor,
Times-Colonist,
Victoria, British Columbia.

I lied. This book doesn't really cover five years. More like six and a bit. Partly because I found a few earlier cartoons worth including because they set the scene, and partly because my cheap publisher Sono Nis Press wanted to pad the book so they could charge you more for it.

I tried to assemble my work chronologically as best I can. However, keeping accurate records and orderly files is a concept alien to me, so don't go asking for your money back if you find I've slipped in a cartoon that appeared June 3rd, 1988 when it should have been June 4th, 1989.

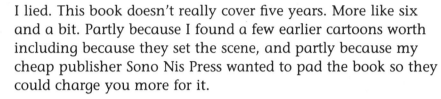

Surrounding municipalities continue to use Victoria's waterfront as a toilet.

Despite the effects of Chernobyl, we are assured that irradiated food is good for us.

There are complaints that artists on the Causeway are ruining Victoria's unique "atmosphere."

After all the interested parties had their input, the design for the new Eaton's Centre is finally approved.

Following a disasterous on-board fire caused by smoking in the washroom, Air Canada bans smoking on its domestic flights.

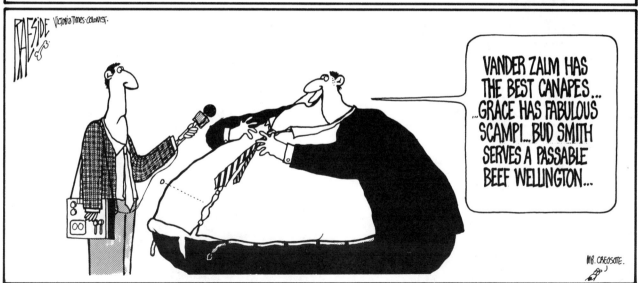

The Socred leadership candidates jammed thousands of dollars down delegates' throats.

As usual, the anti-abortionists don't offer any credible solutions.

1987

The year after EXPO and the first full year of Bill Vander Zalm. At first, most British Columbians thought he was a pretty decent bloke. Eccentric as hell, lived in a papier mâché castle in a religious theme park, but basically OK. Certainly a refreshing change from his boring predecessor, Bill Bennett who by this time had been completely forgotten (until he sold a few Doman shares). A few months into his mandate, there were signs that Zalm was going to be a gold mine of material for me. The first nugget was the creation of a prayer room in the Legislature. Intended to be a place of meditation and quiet devotions, it proved to be a catalyst for special interest groups, atheists and religious flakes. Then Zalm dived into the abortion fight, getting shredded in the process. We also were subjected to friendly fireside chats from Uncle Zalm, giving us advice on everything from moral decay to the best way to prune begonias.

Of course, the Vander Zalm circus wasn't the only interesting event in 1987. Victoria got the Commonwealth Games, Cadillac Fairview came into town with sledgehammers and a grand plan to revitalize downtown Victoria by tearing down our heritage buildings, despite the fact that downtown didn't need revitalizing. It was the year that Rick Hanson came home.

JANUARY 8, 1987   *The latest Health Ministry lunacy . . .*

HOW TO RECOGNIZE SOME OF THE DIFFERENT FACTIONS IN BEIRUT....

ISLAMIC JIHAD

SHIITE AMAL MOVEMENT

HIZBALLAH (PARTY OF GOD)

PALESTINIAN LIBERATION ORGANIZATION

PALESTINIAN REVENGE ORGANIZATION

JUSTICE AND REVENGE FRONT

ISLAMIC RESISTANCE FRONT

SYRIA

...THE POPULAR FRONT 'D FREE UPPER VOLTA...

FEBRUARY 11, 1987

FEBRUARY 20, 1987   *Bay Street is miffed that Vancouver is chosen as an international banking centre.*

APRIL 8, 1987 *The new labour law takes effect.*

APRIL 15, 1987 *The NDP go on the rampage . . . politely.*

MAY 6, 1987   *The legacy of EXPO . . .*

MAY 8, 1987   *The Tories have a weird fear of nakedness in art.*

MAY 24, 1987 *The BC fishing fleet hopes for the day when the Minister of Transport piles his boat onto the rocks in front of an empty lighthouse.*

MAY 25, 1987

JUNE 14, 1987   *Teachers ask for a wee bit more, for a whole lot less.*

JUNE 24, 1987 *Fred Astaire, the world's greatest dancer and a true gentleman, dies.*

JUNE 28, 1987 *As a novel new disservice to the public, posties strike on alternate days.*

AUGUST 9, 1987

AUGUST 23, 1987   *To the delight of city drivers, parking meters were removed from around the Eaton Centre.*
Unfortunately, they were quickly replaced.

SEPTEMBER 2, 1987   *Parts of Island View Beach are designated as "clothing optional."*

SEPTEMBER 3, 1987   *Mulroney hosts the conference of French-speaking nations.*

SEPTEMBER 15, 1987   *Enrollment at universities is at an all-time high. Funding is at an all-time low.*

SEPTEMBER 23, 1987   *The Socreds cry the blues . . . (selectively).*

SEPTEMBER 25, 1987   *A judge complains that newcomers to Canada are eroding our "culture."*

SEPTEMBER 27, 1987   *Government workers lived in mortal terror of where their ministries would end up under Zalm's decentralization plan.*

SEPTEMBER 28, 1987   *Strike #156,321 looms . . .*

OCTOBER 1, 1987   *The Coquihalla opens.*

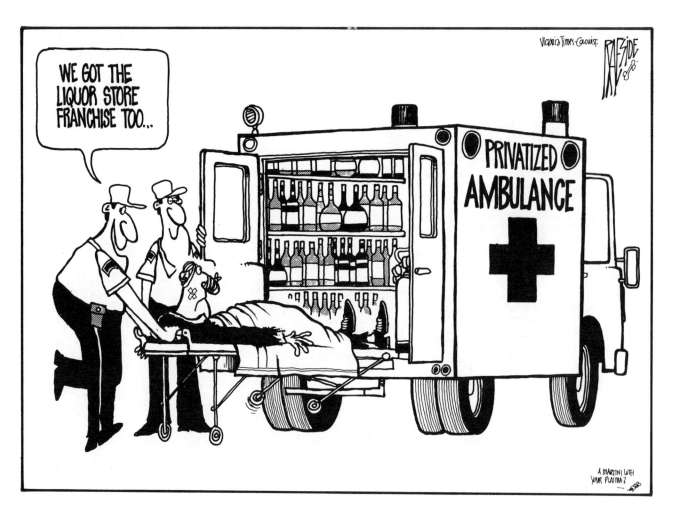

OCTOBER 4, 1987   *Nobody knew what would be privatized next . . .*

OCTOBER 9, 1987 *And upon landing, the monkeys were sent to Siberia.*

OCTOBER 16, 1987   *For once, a Socred cabinet minister tells the truth.*

STEIN VALLEY, BC.

OCTOBER 20, 1987 *A logging road is planned for one of the last wilderness areas in BC.*

OCTOBER 21, 1987   *The stock market plunges . . .*

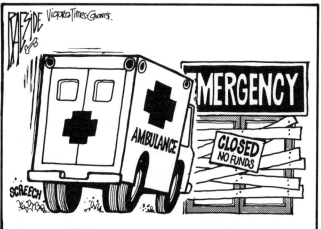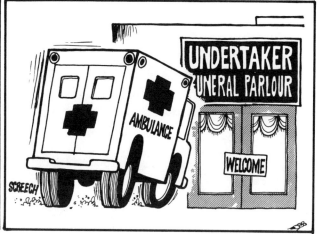

OCTOBER 27, 1987   *As the government cuts health care funding, the number of hospital beds declines in inverse proportion to the number of marble slabs increasing.*

OCTOBER 30, 1987   *The freeways are congested, the skies are crowded and tempers are fraying.*

NOVEMBER 12, 1987   *Victoria gets the Commonwealth Games.*

NOVEMBER 23, 1987   *ICBC penalizes its safe drivers.*

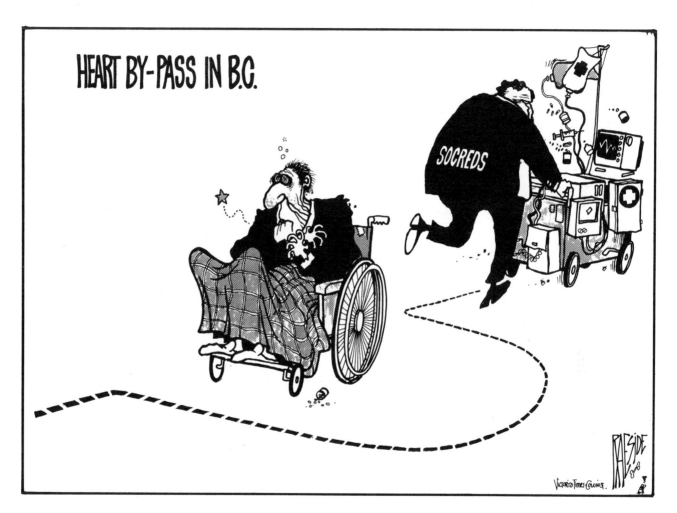

DECEMBER 8, 1987   *Funding for heart patients takes a detour.*

DECEMBER 14, 1987 *Xmas brings lots of neat electronic toys.*

DECEMBER 22, 1987   *Knives are banned from beer parlours. (Personally, I wouldn't go inside some of them without the National Guard to back me up.)*

DECEMBER 23, 1987   *Selective logging.*

1988

The year that Zalm really came out of the closet. Remember regionalization? Decentralization? Complete failures. It's doubtful if most of the sheep that made up his cabinet knew what these words meant, but they followed along blindly with his hare-brained schemes anyway. Scores of civil servants spent needless sleepless nights contemplating a bleak future of filing reports at their new ministry HQ in Spuzzum. It was the year that the Premier's principal secretary, David Poole, disappeared out the back door, considerably richer than he came in. CSIS became the spooks of record. The Environment became fashionable and Couvelier gave away our Maggie.

JANUARY 5, 1988 *The Christmas spirit lasts until Boxing Day.*

JANUARY 6, 1988   *The Canadian prison system's only success seems to be turning petty thugs into hardened criminals.*

JANUARY 8, 1988   *Annual gloatings on the harsh Victoria winters.*

JANUARY 20, 1988   *The US continues its Cruise missile tests in Canada despite peace breaking out around the world.*

FEBRUARY 15, 1988   *Job creation . . . à la Vander Zalm.*

MARCH 2, 1988   *TV evangelists take their crusade out of the arenas and into motel rooms.*

MARCH 6, 1988 *The RCMP are still miffed at the creation of CSIS, depriving them of their most-favoured-spook status.*

MARCH 16, 1988   *The NDP show some baby teeth.*

MARCH 21, 1988   *The pulp mills continue to pollute everything in sight.*

MARCH 24, 1988   *Depositors of failed Principal Trust are visited by those sensitive guys from Revenue Canada.*

MARCH 25, 1988   *Northern Ireland . . . business as usual.*

APRIL 4, 1988   *Surprise, surprise. It turns out the banks have been gouging their customers through dubious service charges.*

APRIL 5, 1988 *Zalm puts his mark on BC . . . again.*

APRIL 8, 1988

APRIL 26, 1988 *John Turner scrambles to fill the Liberal party coffers.*

MAY 22, 1988 *Beautiful downtown Colwood—home of the neon sprawl and the Colwood crawl.*

JUNE 12, 1988   *Jim Keegstra, still spouting his twisted version of the holocaust.*

JUNE 16, 1988   *Your Cruise Director, Bill Vander Zalm.*

JULY 6, 1988   *Things go from worse to worse.*

JULY 20, 1988 *Hard-bargaining Mel gives away what's left of the farm. This cartoon was a collaboration with Peter Lynde, BC's foremost fine artist. (Guess which part of the cartoon is his.)*

JULY 28, 1988 *Great clouds of rust rise up from Esquimalt when the government announces a new minesweeper building program.*

SEPTEMBER 11, 1988   *Victorians consider importing water from Mexico.*

NOVEMBER 21, 1988 *David Poole flees BC politics, taking time only to pack a couple of bags . . .*

DECEMBER 9, 1988 *The "Zalm Disease"—obsessive-compulsive foot-in-mouthitis.*

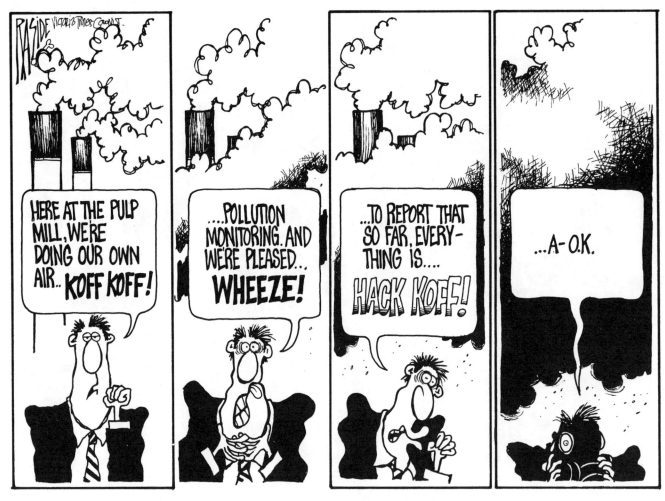

DECEMBER 16, 1988 *Pulp mill operators assure the public that their toxic emissions are at "a safe level."*

DECEMBER 22, 1988   *Remember the office Christmas party of '88? . . . I wish I didn't.*

1989

The year started off well (if you lived in the rest of Canada) by snowing out Victoria's Flower Count: an orgy of excessive gloating about our tropical winters. Torontonians laughed themselves silly at the sight of Victorians plowing into each other on slippery streets and flower counters hunting for daffodils with blowtorches. For the umpteenth time, the long-promised Polar 8 icebreaker was put back in the closet. The *Exxon Valdez* piled into the rocks in Alaska, resulting in calls for sobriety roadblocks in Prince William Sound.

The Tories sliced the lifeline to many communities by closing VIA Rail routes. Vander Zalm decided to run the BC government single-handedly.

By the end of the year, cracks the size of the Rocky Mountain trench were appearing in the Socred Party. Some members were realising that just because someone could play a mean accordion while clog-dancing on tables, it didn't necessarily mean that he could run a province.

JANUARY 23, 1989

JANUARY 25, 1989   *There are only a couple of Multanovas in the province.*

FEBRUARY 3, 1989   *BC's cold snap gets colder . . .*

FEBRUARY 24, 1989   *Mel goes fishing.*

MARCH 2, 1989 *To the horror of the Victoria Chamber of Commerce, Victoria's flower count is snowed out.*

MARCH 5, 1989 *It is hoped that the 1994 Games will be drug-free.*

MARCH 6, 1989

MARCH 13, 1989   *Publication of Salman Rushdie's* Satanic Verses *prompts a predictable response from Tehran.*

APRIL 3, 1989   *This cartoon drew angry letters from the aerosol lobby.*

MAY 12, 1989 *The Polar 8 carrot is put back in Ottawa's fridge.*

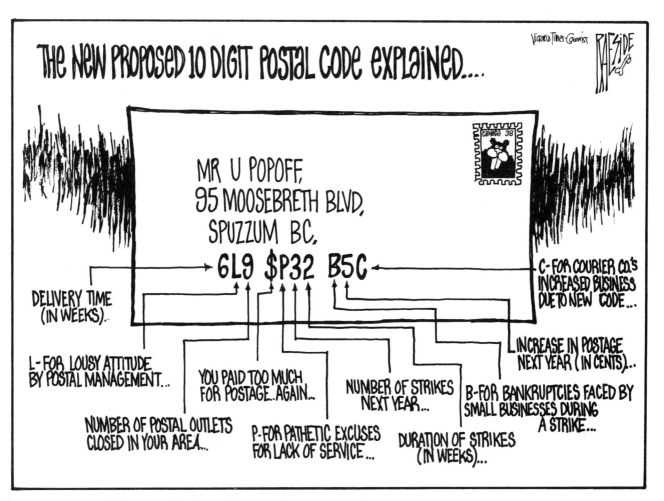

THE NEW PROPOSED 10 DIGIT POSTAL CODE EXPLAINED....

MAY 19, 1989   *If letters with 6 digit codes can take a week to cross town, imagine how long letters with 10 digit codes would take . . .*

MAY 23, 1989 *The aftermath of the Exxon oil spill.*

MAY 26, 1989 *McManning Park?*

JUNE 5, 1989 *Changing times.*

JULY 3, 1989   *Tourism BC comes up with a hokey new ad campaign, picturing deer grazing in a lush BC forest . . . Everyone wondered where they found the forest.*

THE LAST SPIKE....

JULY 7, 1989   *The Feds pole-axe most of Via Rail's routes.*

JULY 11, 1989 *The RCMP allow turbans for its Sikh officers.*

JULY 28, 1989

AUGUST 18, 1989

AUGUST 30, 1989   *. . . with optional printing press inside.*

OCTOBER 2, 1989

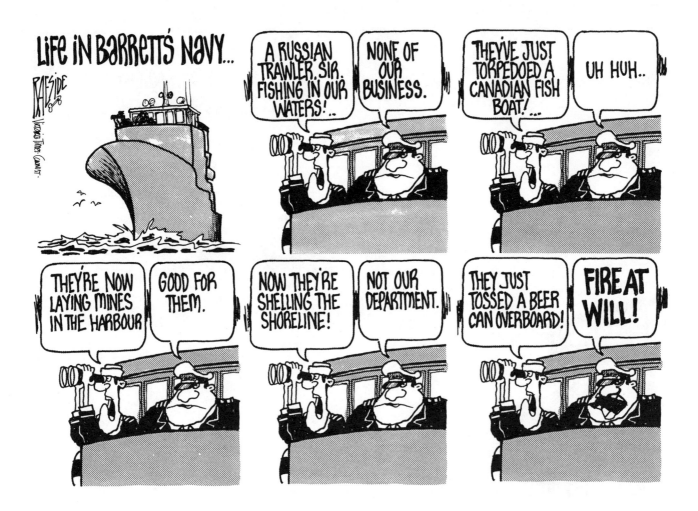

OCTOBER 18, 1989   *MP Dave Barrett comes up with a scheme to turn Canada's navy into an environmental force, if the NDP is elected.*

OCTOBER 19, 1989

OCTOBER 27, 1989   *At the annual Socred convention, delegates were desperately trying not to notice the smell.*

NOVEMBER 3, 1989 *Next, waterslides at Chernobyl.*

NOVEMBER 6, 1989   *The cemetery of Socred brilliant schemes is filling up.*

NOVEMBER 13, 1989   *As usual, the elderly and the poor are most affected by lack of affordable housing. As usual, local and provincial governments don't give a damn.*

NOVEMBER 15, 1989

1990

Gotta be one of the weirdest years in BC. Almost as if every day was a full moon. Half the roads were blocked by protesting Indians and the other half by protesting environmentalists. Mulroney rammed the GST through, despite the majority of Canadians rejecting it. The Senate woke up from its 100-year coma to do battle against the tax but was foiled by Mulroney stacking the Senate with Tory hacks who overwhelmed the Liberal hacks. The Meech Lake Accord was cobbled together by the PM and the premiers, none of whom had the slightest idea what Canada meant to the people who had elected them. Fortunately, it was a native Indian, Elijah Harper, who had the guts to stand up to the Feds and scuttle the accord. Stena cruise lines packed up their toys and left Victoria. As usual, Zalm celebrated Christmas with his back to the wall.

JANUARY 25, 1990   *The Feds come up with new warnings for cigarette packages.*

JANUARY 26, 1990 *Quebec demands "distinct society" status.*

JANUARY 28, 1990 *Michael Wilson's pathetic attempts to justify the GST in the Commons is met with predictable results.*

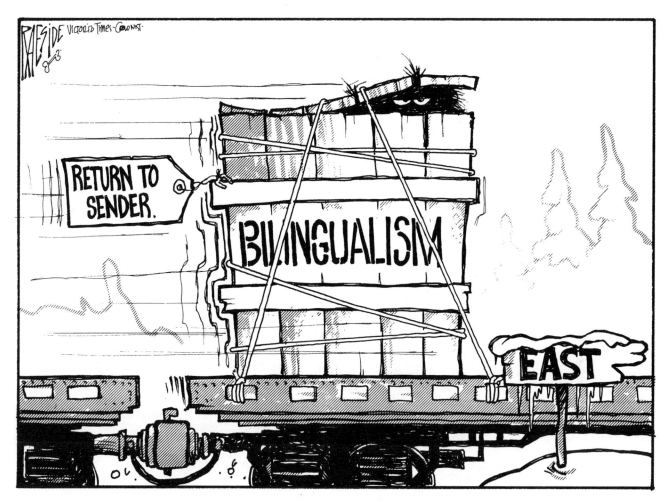

FEBRUARY 9, 1990   *Various local councils repeal bilingualism.*

THE CRY OF THE LOON ....

FEBRUARY 28, 1990   *Yet another oil spill hits the beaches.*

MARCH 9, 1990   *The National Gallery blows a fortune of our money on a piece of art nobody could understand—by an American artist.*

MARCH 18, 1990   *Air Canada pulls out of BC's capital.*

MARCH 21, 1990   *Mulroney's largesse on the international stage knows no bounds . . . or sense.*

APRIL 6, 1990 *Reasonable accommodation, especially in Vancouver, is becoming more and more expensive, as houses are torn down for apartments . . . and apartments go condo.*

APRIL 15, 1990   *CRD engineers decide that this small pristine lake south of Victoria's Hartland Avenue garbage dump would be better if it was drained and filled with garbage. (Starting with the minutes of CRD meetings?)*

APRIL 16, 1990 *The Western Canada Wilderness Committee comes up with a cunning plan . . .*

MAY 6, 1990   *Retailers discover the $$$ in going green.*

MAY 7, 1990   *The provincial Environment Ministry goes a milquetoast blitz.*

MAY 31, 1990 *The Socreds indulge in their favourite sport—doctor bashing.*

JUNE 11, 1990

JUNE 15, 1990   *The nine-month monsoon season winds up.*

JUNE 20, 1990 *Reminiscent of Tiananmen Square, native leader Elijah Harper stops the Meech Lake tanks from rolling across Canada.*

JULY 6, 1990 *Apparently, some perfectly healthy (well, maybe slightly overweight) MLAs are hogging seats on government planes, forcing some medical patients to make alternate travel plans.*

JULY 13, 1990 *People would be more sympathetic to the native population if they mowed their lawns and stuck pink flamingos in their front yards.*

JULY 26, 1990   *Vander Zalm pursues a burglar at Fantasy Gardens and ends up apprehending his bike.*

INdiaN WEaPONS THROUGH THE ages...

Victoria Times-Colonist

Tomahawk: **Bow & arrow:** **Musket:** **La-Z-Boy:**

AUGUST 22, 1990 *A lot of people were upset with me over this cartoon. They thought I was calling Indians lazy boys. Oddly enough, only white people complained. The Indians appreciated the message.*

AUGUST 26, 1990 *Parking spots in Victoria are becoming as scarce as morals in the legislature.*

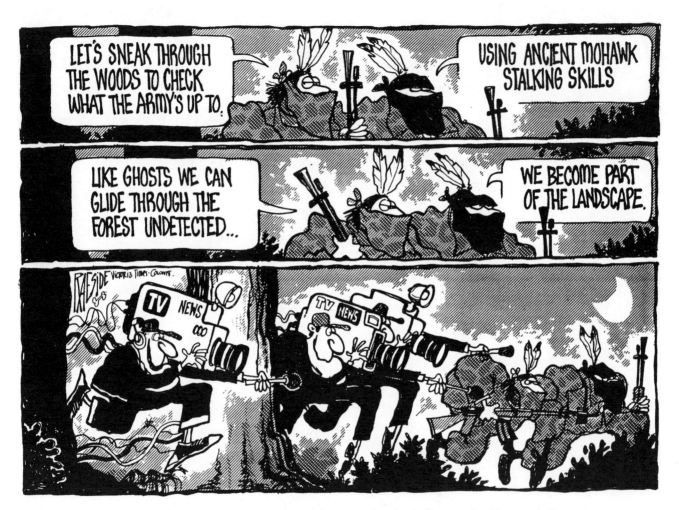

SEPTEMBER 7, 1990   *At times, the media outnumber the Indians at the Oka standoff.*

SEPTEMBER 14, 1990   *As another cabinet minister goes down, another lottery game pops up.*

SEPTEMBER 26, 1990   *To get your message out in the summer of 1990, all you needed was a lawn chair and a road.*

OCTOBER 7, 1990 *The TV show "A Current Affair" takes a hidden camera into the sleaze-infested Vancouver Stock Exchange.*

OCTOBER 9, 1990 *The great Senate GST debate rages . . . as if paying an extra 7% would have any real effect on those overpaid layabouts.*

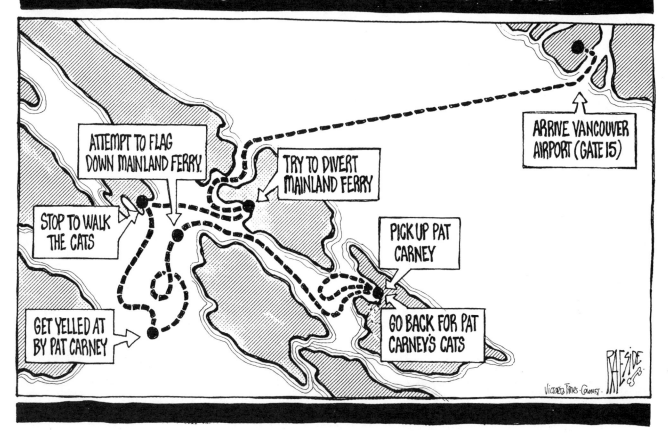

OCTOBER 11, 1990 *Senator Pat Carney, in her usual quiet, refined way, tries to commandeer a BC Ferry, so she can catch a flight to Ottawa. Ottawa is delighted she misses it—BC isn't.*

OCTOBER 15, 1990 *Wildlife officers go high-tech to nail low-life game poachers.*

OCTOBER 21, 1990

OCTOBER 22, 1990 *Doctors continue their battle with the Socreds for higher fees.*

OCTOBER 25, 1990 *The latest poll comes out. The NDP is #1, the Liberals #2 . . . the Tories, as usual, are in the basement.*

OCTOBER 26, 1990   *Michael Wilson's timing is impeccable.*

OCTOBER 28, 1990 *Zalm and Mulroney fall over themselves to avoid dealing with Indian land claims.*

NOVEMBER 12, 1990   *The municipal elections bring out a stampede of born-again-hug-a-spotted-owl environmentaloids.*

NOVEMBER 15, 1990 *Stena Lines slinks back to Sweden. Too bad they don't take Couvelier, who had started the whole mess, with them.*

NOVEMBER 18, 1990 *The morning after the municipal elections.*

NOVEMBER 25, 1990 *BC government clerks reel from the generosity of their employer.*

DECEMBER 2, 1990   *Zalm spends 50% of his time lighting fires, the other 50% putting them out.*

DECEMBER 9, 1990 *The Tories gut the CBC.*

DECEMBER 10, 1990 *The US government considers a plan to charge Canadians $5.00 to visit the States.*

DECEMBER 12, 1990 *Some Socred constituency chiefs make strong hints to Zalm regarding his leadership abilities.*

DECEMBER 20, 1990 *Much to the delight of the rest of Canada, Victoria endures a cold snap.*

1991

We thought 1990 was tumultuous. Jeepers, those were halcyon days compared to '91. The Berlin Wall came down, the Red Army retreated, arms treaties were signed, the failed coup in Russia spurred the Baltic States to freedom, Quebec threatened to separate (again), the Spicer Commission spent its way across Canada, we went to war to defend a tinpot dictatorship that just happens to be sitting on a lake of oil. That was in the real world. Back home, Zalm finished digging his hole and jumped in.

I was sorry to see him go. Mostly because he was so easy to draw and he did most of my work for me. Zalm came up with stuff I couldn't dream of in a million years. Although I knew the day would come when he'd go, I watched in horror as he resigned. I am sure he did it just to spite the

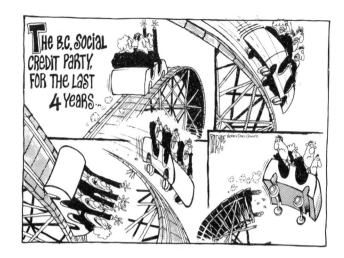

editorial cartoonists who have been feeding off him like cowbirds for the last few years. With Vander Zalm went my dreams of buying a new car.

With events getting more bizarre as the years go on, it is comforting to know there will always be a source of topics to draw on. Besides, who knows, Zalm may make a comeback in the year 2000.

I'd vote for him.

JANUARY 2, 1991   *Mulroney and Bourassa take turns in trashing the country.*

JANUARY 3, 1991 *Retailers despair at ever reconfigurating their cash registers.*

JANUARY 4, 1991 *The* Huron *sails for the Gulf War.*

JANUARY 9, 1991 *Not many people notice that highways maintenance was privatized—until the first snowfall.*

JANUARY 31, 1991   *Of course, there's no guarantee they'll actually have any skills if they graduate.*

FEBRUARY 10, 1991 *Bourassa threatens to take Quebec out of Canada. Many Canadians offer to help pack her bags.*

FEBRUARY 17, 1991   *The Premier's office was running out of carpets to sweep the dirt under.*

FEBRUARY 24, 1991   *Victoria Council slams some guy with a few chickens in his back yard, citing noise by-laws.*

FEBRUARY 26, 1991 *Iraqi government radio is a little slow to report Iraq's spectacular defeat.*

FEBRUARY 27, 1991   *Michael Wilson is at a loss to explain the lethargy in Canada's economy.*

MARCH 6, 1991   *Tourists flock to gape at highly intelligent marine mammals forced to perform degrading acts in pools not much larger than Jacuzzis.*

Mike Harcourt's Range of Emotions....

Victoria Times-Colonist.

RAESIDE

THOUGHTFUL	ANGRY	HAPPY	OUTRAGED	OVERJOYED
DEVASTATED	REFLECTIVE	FURIOUS	AMUSED	IRATE	STEAMED
TICKED OFF	EUPHORIC	ON THE WAR PATH	MAD·AS·HELL	SERENE	FRENZIED

MARCH 10, 1991   *"Iron" Mike.*

MARCH 14, 1991   *The CRD and local councils continue to ignore our beaches which are knee-deep in sh*t.*

MARCH 15, 1991   *One consolation is that there is no one to hate and no promises to keep.*

MARCH 24, 1991 *This cartoon prompted a call from a Guelph, Ontario, newspaper columnist demanding to know what I had against Guelph.*

MARCH 28, 1991

MARCH 31, 1991 *I watched in dismay, as I saw one quarter of my income go out the window.*

MAY 2, 1991   *The Socreds are beginning to think that Count Von Vander Zalm is immortal . . .*

MAY 30, 1991   *Much to the party's delight, Zalm goes on vacation. However, he does come back.*

MAY 31, 1991   *Cross-border shopping takes on the status of a mass exodus.*

JUNE 5, 1991   *Ottawa lets the tax-collecting provinces loose on Canadians returning from cross-border shopping trips.*

JUNE 17, 1991 *After the Iraq war, Americans dance in the streets as the Kurds are bombed by Saddam.*

The mike harcourt Doll...

.... WIND IT UP AND IT DOES NOTHING.

JUNE 24, 1991   *All this for $85,873 per year (no GST).*

JULY 2, 1991   *The media find themselves in the embarrassing situation of making the leadership candidates' lives easier.*

JULY 4, 1991 *The Tories embrace the Spicer Report.*

JULY 17, 1991 *Gorbachev goes to the G-7 to ask for financial aid.*

JULY 18, 1991 *The task of selecting a new leader begins.*

ISN'T IT COMFORTING...

Victoria Times-Colonist.

RAESIDE

GRACE COU... ALL THE WAY WITH RITA J.!

GRACE NORT

RITA
MR. PEANUT
MEL
ZALM
GRACEGRACE
NORT
RITARITARI
G
MELMEL

GRACIE J

.....TO THINK THAT 1,900 OF THESE WILL PICK THE NEXT LEADER OF OUR PROVINCE...

JULY 19, 1991   *There is some truth to the old saying—you get the leaders you deserve.*

JULY 21, 1991   *It's official—Rita is voted the next Socred leader.*

JULY 22, 1991   *Winnipeg suffers a mosquito invasion.*

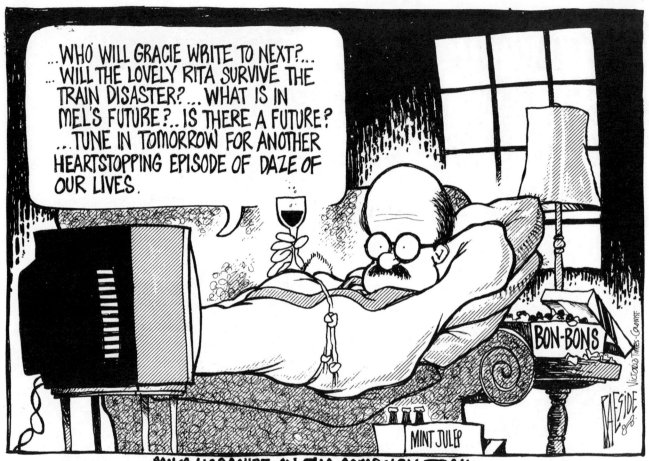

MIKE HARCOURT ON THE CAMPAIGN TRAIL....

JULY 26, 1991 *The NDP slip into their robes, pop another chockie into their mouths and settle down to watch the Socreds self-destruct.*

JULY 28, 1991 *Rita indulges in a little NDP/Ontario bashing.*

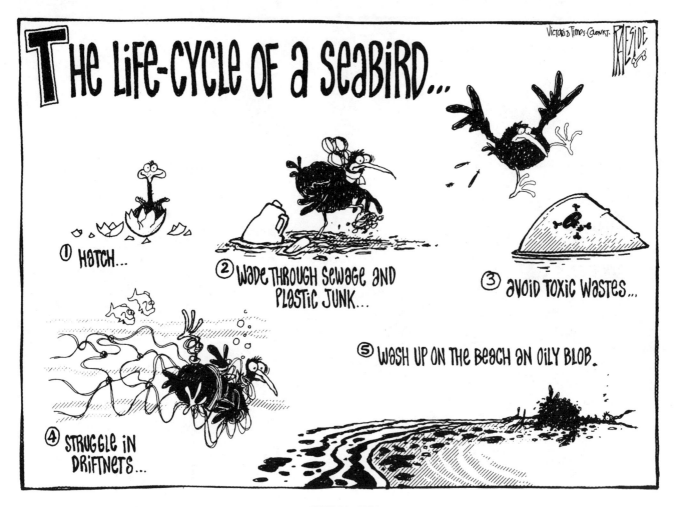

JULY 31, 1991

AUGUST 2, 1991 *Tourism was down and nobody was sure why.*

AUGUST 22, 1991   *The Russian coup that failed.*

AUGUST 26, 1991   *The Whistler Premier's Conference on the eve of an election.*

AUGUST 30, 1991   *The triumphant return from the Whistler Premier's Conference.*

SEPTEMBER 4, 1991   *Mail strike #396,149.*

SEPTEMBER 20, 1991 *The 1991 election is called.*

Of all the charities around, Amnesty International and Hospice always get my support. They deal with the unpleasant sides of life that most of us try to ignore.

Acknowledgements

Thanks to . . . my mother and father, who for so many years have put up with my bizarre work habits, irritating eccentricities, questionable humour and sloppy dress. *Don Vipond*, my editor, who put up with all of the above, but had the added burden of having to correct my spelling and field irate phone calls. *My brother*, the logger, who had to bite his tongue every time I skewered his profession. *My aunt* who was always there to give artistic advice. *My editor at Sono Nis Press* who went gray hounding me to put this book together in time. *All the newspaper readers* who have supported me for all these years by buying the newspaper.

You are all held responsible.